THE DRUNK SONNETS

The Drunk Sonnets
© 2013 Daniel Bailey

Published by Magic Helicopter Press
Northampton, MA
www.magichelicopterpress.com

ISBN: 978-0-9841406-0-2

2 4 6 8 9 7 5 3 1 0
First edition: October 2009
Second edition: January 2013

Titles are set in HVD Poster (by Hannes von Döhren); text in Crimson (by Sebastian Kosch)

Cover design: Chelsea Martin
Book design: Mike Young

THE DRUNK SONNETS

Daniel Bailey

MAGIC HELICOPTER PRESS

Northampton, MA

CONTENTS

14 ON THE DRUNK SONNETS
SEAN LOVELACE

1. *You have to be always drunk. That's all there is to it—it's the only way. So as not to feel the horrible burden of time that breaks your back and bends you to the earth, you have to be continually drunk.*

But on what? Wine, poetry or virtue, as you wish. But be drunk.
—Charles Baudelaire

2. (Cracks open bottle. Primes engine.) Mr. Bailey says he wrote these poems while imbibing ("I was pretty drunk for some of them, a little drunk for others"), and why can't I do the same? Ah, beer and poetry. The bubbles rising, the words off the page. All the numberless forms of necessary intoxication. I can already feel my synapses pop and crackle.

3. What are the criteria for the sonnet? Fourteen lines, yes. Ten syllables, I suppose, mostly. (Many modern sonneters have bent the form to need as one would an old clothes hanger, creating inverted sonnets, word sonnets, curtails, caudates, clusterfucks, and so on). Rhyme? Could be. Meter? Well, most of us don't even fully understand meter. (It is the rhythmic ticking in your temples after 11 beers. It is the ceiling fan above your putrid head the blue morning

you wake naked on the kitchen floor.) It should proceed naturally (like beer). It should contain no trickery or special effects (like beer). It should be fresh (like beer) and should sustain (like beer). It should present a situation/problem and reflect upon. There might be, along the foamy dregs of the form, *a turn*.

[go to drunk sonnet 11

go to drunk sonnet 32

for example]

Mr. Bailey, on the sonnet form: "It allows for a huge thing to be compressed into a small area, which is why I had to write so many of them. It allows for prolificness. It requires conciseness. and somehow the last two lines always force you into a place where you're not sure what's going to happen, but the chance of goodness is favorable, usually. Seeing the end of the poem raises the stakes. It causes drama within the heart. It raises the blood pressure. I'm pretty sure it causes fever. Recklessness disappears. When you have the end in sight, you know what you have to do."

(Note: *Prolificness* is not an actual word, as far as I can tell, but I've never met a real poet who gave a damn about such matters.)

4. What is the question *The Drunk Sonnets* asks? What is the situation/problem? What is the horrible burden for the construction

to address? Are you asking me? I'm asking you. OK, I'll give you five right off my head, then leave lined spaces for you to write in three more. Ready?

- Push or pull?
- Coughing or crying?
- Is the simile a type of god?
- Is it OK if I don't watch myself tonight?
- Mirror or warning?
- ____________________
- ____________________
- ____________________

[Note: I hope it's clear I'm not doing all the heavy lifting in this introduction. Go drink a beer. Go read the poems. Why? *Why?*]

5. Did you just ask why? Because you cannot describe the feeling of drinking quality ale. You cannot describe a quality poem, not really. The only way to do so—with either style of intoxication, or both together—would be to recreate the actual beer, the actual poem, the actual situation simultaneously in that one moment of existence. This is impossible. But, amazingly, you can try. The poet, the brewer—they are offering you an opportunity. Listen: You are reading the book, *The Drunk Sonnets*. Certainly you have some access to alcohol. So attempt to create what I am feeling now. Tonight. Stupefy! Go!

(Note: Never trust an interpretation of a poem as that poem. Same with beer. To look outside the experience is foolish.)

6. *Thus the large part of all that is produced in our world is accomplished in a non-sober condition.* —Leo Tolstoy

7. Virtue, Baudelaire says. But what the fuck is virtue? What we want to see is less abstract words. The more concrete. The better. Things. See *The Drunk Sonnets*, for example, the book you now grip like a pin-pulled grenade.

[go to drunk sonnet 26
for example]

8. Note: I certainly hope this second edition has a more appropriate cover than the first edition. (I haven't seen the new edition; it isn't out yet at this writing.) As I've noted elsewhere, the first cover resembled a pastel vat of popcorn. I prefer a cover of Mr. Bailey vomiting in a Muncie, Indiana alleyway. Or onto a crow or some other large bird. A crow pinned to the ground by a tennis shoe. Or maybe something more abstract, like a muskrat blowing into a Breathalyzer, in the moonlight down by an abandoned Chevrolet factory runoff pipe? (The local White River has many, many runoff pipes and I know for a fact Mr. Bailey has swum, while intoxicated, in the heavily polluted White River at least once.) Fuck, I don't know. I'm feeling a little buzz now. An effective book cover is a complex endeavor. (Hold up, I have to get another beer.) Readers: If the cover

of this book you're holding resembles a vat of popcorn, the editors did not alter the cover. As is their prerogative. Just saying, you know. Popcorn.

[Publisher's Note: The first cover was done by Chelsea Martin, and it's actually not a vat of popcorn but a bucket of chicken from a relatively major chicken bucket producing institution. I love it. Bless Mr. Lovelace's heart and liver, but he's totally wrong on this one. When I first emailed Chelsea, I said: *so for the cover i am thinking THE DRUNK SONNETS in large letters, dan's name somewhere stylishly, and a whale of some sort* and then I sent another email that said *or wolves, tigers, sharks, tasmanian devils, Malaysian sun bears, or barracudas, dan says.* Chelsea sent us the bucket. I was like: of course. When Dan saw it, he emailed me and said: *yessss, that is great. is that a bucket of ice cream?* Chelsea also did the cover of the second edition, the one you're holding, which is—obviously—a bottle of antacids.]

9. *Your days are your sonnets.* — Oscar Wilde.

10. Sonnet as a six-pack. Ah, I see your logic. As containing, as narrative, as beginning, middle, ending, with a certain flow, yet the flow changes as we wade through the 6 pack, as we literally *change,* fall into intoxication, are led from *beer* to *beer* to *beer.*

11. Or as engine of juxtaposition? I now direct you to the poem, Drunk Sonnet # 18. Go ahead, find and read the thing, I'll wait. See what I mean? Forget about me, OK? YOU go get a beer. YOU go read Drunk Sonnet # 18. That's what I keep telling YOU. Do you see it? Read it again. Do you see it? That's juxtaposition. This with that, leading to a new *thing*. A *thing* behind the *thing*. That's the beauty of the technique.

[Note: I once read Drunk Sonnet # 18 aloud and then shot the poem with an assault rifle. If interested, you can see the act by Googling "drunk sonnet 18 video." You'll find it.]

12. Years ago I first saw Mr. Bailey in an undergraduate college classroom at Ball State University. I remember him, the same way I remember the one or two students per semester that I think, "Hmm. They might be serious. They might have a chance." Was he drinking? I have no idea. Students often do drink in class: I once had to liberate a vodka and OJ from a sophomore of the University of Alabama since he wouldn't stop passing the tall sloshing cup along the entire back row. But with Mr. Bailey, I noticed no obvious signs. What do I remember? He seemed fidgety, aware, observant, flustered for moments then calm, a bit tired-of-it-all, then suddenly very engaged, a bit like he was itching, or maybe bleeding, most likely itching or bleeding words. Some mornings Mr. Bailey arrived for class looking like he'd had four hours of sleep. Some mornings like he'd had none. So, you know, a poet.

[drunk sonnet # 41

For example

13. _All you have is what you have and that's what will come out if you treat it right and that is a beautiful thing._ — Daniel Bailey

14. The eye: What beauty does Mr. Bailey behold? Are you drunk yet? I'm certainly on my way. (Oddly, it's a beer from Breckenridge Brewery, of Colorado, a state now home to one Mr. Daniel Bailey.) And it seems poetry expands now (cracking open, like a geode) for me, its beauty almost tangible, and blossoming (songs will do the same while intoxicated, as you well know). Because they glimmer, I grab:

- PILE OF DUCK BLANKETS (sonnet # 28)
- BIRTHING A GHOST (sonnet # 19)
- MY EYES SCALED UP LIKE TWIN LIZARD FETUSES (sonnet # 48)

What do you grab? Go right ahead. Let's forget the listing, the lined spacing, the rational mind; go ahead and scribble all over this introduction, this page, this book. _Sprawl. Fall about. Get drunk!_ Read this book now. Listen to Mr. Baudelaire now, to Mr. Bailey now. Drunk, in all its connotations. That's sort of the point of all this, you understand?

DRuNK SONNET 1

I'M A LITTLE HUNGRY BUT DRUNK
I WANT FORGIVENESS IN A BEEHIVE
LIKE A DOG WITH THE BENDS IN THE ARCTIC
AND COVERED IN ICE FURS

MY FIRST PRAYER TO GOD WENT
I DON'T KNOW IF I'M DOING THIS RIGHT
MY LAST PRAYER TO GOD WENT
I KNOW FOR A FACT I'M NOT DOING THIS RIGHT

I CAN'T SLEEP AT NIGHT AND AT DAY I DON'T WANT AWAKE
AND A BODY THAT RUSTS INTO HARD AND AND UNBELIEVABLE
I WILL BE NOT ALIVE FOREVER EXCEPT FOR THE DRY BED

MY HANDS ARE TOO SMALL TO CARRY WHATEVER THIS IS
ACTUALLY, A HABIT OF DOLPHINS THAT LIVE IN CAPTIVITY
TO EAT FISH OUT OF BUCKETS AND SLEEP IN THE SALT AND THE WATER

DRuNK SONNET 2

BODIES FLOAT WITHOUT BALLAST
AND I GUESS THAT'S WHY I'M HERE
AND I GUESS THAT'S WHY YOU'RE HERE
AND WHY, HARDLY, I STILL LOVE YOU

WE FORGOT THE ROCKS AND
WE FORGOT THE CEMENT AND
THE HEAVY SHIT IS SOMEWHERE ELSE
BUT I WANT TO BREATHE UNDERWATER

LIKE BUBBLES I WANT TO TOUCH YOUR DEAD FACE
WITH MY DEAD FACE TO LICK YOU WITH AIR
THE WEEKENDS ARE GONE AND SO ARE THE NIGHTS

I DON'T EVEN REMEMBER THE TIMES THAT I LOVED YOU
BUT I DO AND I WANT TO REMEMBER THEM LIKE I DRANK TOO MUCH
AND WHAT EVEN HAPPENED I DON'T EVEN KNOW

DRUNK SONNET 3

PRACTICALLY, I AM MAKING IT THROUGH LIFE
LIKE THE GROUND KEEPS PAYING ME TO WALK ON IT
WITH THE HUMILIATION OF KNOWING ITS STRENGTH
AGAINST MY WEIGHT AND I CANNOT WIN OR BREAK THE SURFACE

SOMETIMES IN LIFE SOMEONE SAYS HELLO
AND YOU ARE ALL, I DON'T KNOW, PLEASE
AND, I NEED YOU, COME HERE, WHERE ARE YOU
AND, I KNOW HOW YOU FEEL ...

THERE'S THIS A/C UNIT AND IT'S COVERED WITH BOTTLES
AND I AM TRYING TO MAKE SENSE AT ALL, YOU KNOW
AND TRAINS KEEP WHISTLING IN THE DISTANCE

BUT WHAT HAPPENS IS I KEEP LOOKING AWAY
AND LOOKING AWAY IS ANOTHER THING
AND ANOTHER THING IS MAYBE BETTER RIGHT NOW

DRUNK SONNET 4

COME ON, YOU PEOPLE, EVERYTHING IS OK
THE CHILDREN ARE ASLEEP AND THE DOGS ARE ASLEEP
AND MY STOMACH AND HEAD ARE CONNECTED IN THIS WAY
THAT I CAN HEAR THOUGHTS LIKE PIZZA CHOKING BEER

OBVIOUSLY, THE ROOM IS SHAKING A LITTLE
TELL ME IT'S NOT, YOU ARE A LIAR IT SHAKES, BIG TIME
I AM CONTENT AND THAT IS GOOD, BUT LONELY
I REMEMBER HOW THE BODY TASTES AND HOW HARDLY GONE IT IS

TOMORROW I WILL WAKE UP AND GO TO WORK FOR A TRAINING
I WILL LISTEN AND I WILL NOD MY HEAD AND THAT'S THAT
I'LL LEAVE WORK AND LEAVE WORK AND LEAVE WORK

AND I'LL LEAVE WORK AND EAT SOME CHEAP FOOD AND I KNOW
MY HOURS WILL CONTRIBUTE TO MY MONETARY WORTH AND I WISH
I COULD BUY YOU SOMETHING FOR YOUR TIME BUT IT'S GONE

DRUNK SONNET 5

WHERE IS MY LIFE, I THINK A DONE THING
THAT I WANT TO CONTINUE FOREVER AND REMEMBER
COMPLETELY DRUNKFUL AND BEAUTIFUL TO BOOT, AS THEY SAY
WHAT HAPPENS NOW IS WE CONTINUE SEPARATELY AND THAT'S THAT

IT'S LIKE YOU ARE THERE AND I AM HERE
AND I DON'T KNOW WHERE THERE IS BUT HERE IS IRRELEVANT
THE CAPITAL BUILDING IS CRUSHING ME FROM ACROSS THE CITY
AND THE SENATORS ARE ALL GETTING MASHED UP GOOD

CAN YOU BELIEVE THAT PEOPLE WANT LIFE TO MEAN SOMETHING
I WISH I WERE THE MOSS ON THE TREE STUMP IN ANOTHER STATE
AND WE NEVER ENDED UP SEEING EACH OTHER

I CAN'T BELIEVE THAT WHAT I DRINK EVERY NIGHT CAN MAKE ME FEEL
ANY DIFFERENT, AND I THINK WE'LL BE GONE FOREVER RIGHT NOW
I AM GONE AND YOU ARE GONE AND THAT IS IT

DRuNK SONNET 6

MY BODY WANTS SOMETHING MORE THAN IT GETS
MY STOMACH SAYS HUNGRY PIZZA JAMBALAYA SANDWICH
MY HEART WANTS BLOOD TO FEED ITS ACHING WORTHLESS
MY RIB JUST WANTS TO SIT THERE AND PROTECT

WHAT ABOUT THE LIVER, THAT SHITTY BUTTWAD
THE LIVER WANTS A NEW LIFE INSIDE A CHRISTIAN WOMAN
BODY, COME ON, I CANNOT COMPLETE THIS INSPECTION
I AM GOING DOWN—YOU TOO—WE ARE KAMIKAZED, BIG TIME

I DIDN'T MEAN TO DO THAT, BUT I AM HUNGRY
THE CARPET WANTS FEET, I AM HONEST AND DEAD
GOD IS A HORRIBLE DISEASE THAT I INHERITED

IF I COULD LIVE INSIDE YOU AND YOU INSIDE ME
THEN THAT WOULD BE IDEAL—DISTANCE IS NOT NECESSARY
MY CAR JUST EXPLODED AND NO SHIT EVER EVER HAPPENED

DRuNK SONNET 7

EVERYTHING AROUND ME IS SHAKING A LITTLE
LIFE IS HORRIBLE AND A GREAT THING TO DEAL WITH
RIGHT NOW I'M TRYING TO GO ON AND IT'S WORKING
ALL I HAVE TO DO IS KEEP BREATHING AND KEEP BEATING

GOD, THIS IS AMAZING, THIS CHAIR, THIS AIR, THESE HANDS
MY BODY FEELS LIKE A SHIT GETTING SUCKED DOWN THE DRAIN
MY BROTHER IS AWESOME AND LETS ME STAY HERE AND YOU ARE NOT HERE
EVERYONE TRIES SO HARD AT EVERYTHING THAT IT'S LIKE HELL YES

I AM TRYING FOR YOU—DO YOU REALIZE THAT?
EVERYTHING IS A LITTLE DIFFERENT SINCE THE SWAMPS FORMED
IT SMELLED A LITTLE LIKE GRASS FERMENTED AND DEAD

WHEN YOUR HEAD GETS RIPPED OFF YOUR SPINE GOES TOO
TO GROW ANOTHER BODY WOULD BE A GOOD IDEA
I WANT JUST WANT A NEW EVERYTHING WITH IT

DRuNK SONNET 8

I WANT TO LOVE BUT PLEASE LET ME KNOW
HOW IS IT THAT I CAN YOU CAN EVEN EXIST NOW
I JUST FELT THE ALCOHOL IN MY FEET
MY HEART HAS A LOT INSIDE IT I THINK, EVEN STILL

IF EVERYONE IS OK THEN WHY AM I NOT
IT'S OK TO CRY A LITTLE, I THINK, JUST CRY
I THINK I WANT TO EAT YOUR SMILE TONIGHT
I THINK THERE'S SOMETHING IN IT TO KEEP ME ALIVE

I'M LOOKING AT THIS SLEEPING CAT RIGHT NOW
AND HE JUST SHIFTED A LITTLE AND IT WAS NICE
AND THE OCEAN'S FLOOR IS SO FAR AWAY

SINKING TOGETHER WOULD BE A COMMITMENT
AND RISING TOGETHER AN EVEN BIGGER ONE
BUT I THINK THAT ALL THAT WATER IS TOO MUCH

DRUNK SONNET 9

I'M GLAD THAT YOU'RE SILL ALIVE AND DOING WELL
I'D HATE TO LIVE IN A WORLD WHERE YOU DON'T EXIST
I CAN SAY THAT HONESTLY, AND I'M GLAD I DON'T HAVE TO LIE
IF YOU KNOW ME, AND I THINK YOU DO, YOU KNOW I'M NOT A LIAR

EXCEPT FOR WHEN EVERYTHING GOES WRONG IN LIFE
AND I HAVE TO BACK AWAY FOR A LITTLE WHILE
INTO ANOTHER CORNER OF LIFE WHERE I'LL SAY ANYTHING
TO MAKE YOU BELIEVE ME RIGHT NOW

SOMETIMES THE ONLY THINGS THAT WORK OUT ARE MUSCLES
AND I GOT VERY FEW OF THOSE AND IT HURTS
TO SEE YOU DOING WELL AT ALL

OR TO IMAGINE YOU DOING WELL, BUT YOU ARE
BUT I MAKE IT THROUGH THE DAYS
AND THAT'S OK, I THINK, AT LEAST I CAN DO PUSH UPS

DRuNK SONNET 10

THE AIRPORT IS A TERRIBLE PLACE TO EXIST
THE GROCERY STORE IS A TERRIBLE PLACE TO EXIST
PETSMART IS A TERRIBLE PLACE TO EXIST
THE THAI PLACE IS A TERRIBLE PLACE TO EXIST

MY OWN BED IS A TERRIBLE PLACE TO EXIST
INSIDE MY CAR IS A TERRIBLE PLACE TO EXIST
ALL THESE STREETS, THIS CITY, THIS STATE
THIS COUNTRY IS A TERRIBLE PLACE TO EXIST

IN FRONT OF THIS TV IS A TERRIBLE PLACE TO EXIST
IN THIS BODY IS A TERRIBLE PLACE TO EXIST
IN THIS AIR IS A TERRIBLE PLACE TO EXIST

I'M THINKING ABOUT EVOLUTION AND THE WAY WE CHANGE
AND HOW LONG IT WILL BE BEFORE I HAVE A TAIL AGAIN
AND I CAN STUFF IT BETWEEN MY LEGS

DRUNK SONNET 11

MY DRUNK IS GOING AWAY AND IT'S A LITTLE HOT
LIKE I AM IN A DESERT AND LICKING THE SAND
BENEATH THE SAND TO STAY COOL THOUGH IT'S WRONG
AND THIS WILL JUST MAKE THINGS WORSE

I CAN'T TALK RIGHT NOW WITH MY MOUTH FULL OF SAND
IF YOU WANT TO TALK LEAVE A MESSAGE AND I WILL RESPOND
AT A BETTER TIME I HOPE YOU UNDERSTAND
BUT I UNDERSTAND IF YOU NEVER DO

AND IF I NEVER DO
AND IF WHAT WAS GOOD WAS NOT REALLY GOOD
BUT WE WERE TRYING TOO HARD TO BE GOOD

SOMETIMES I CAN FEEL A CAMEL LICKING MY BACK
AND WHEN I TURN AROUND I AM SUDDENLY SLEEPING
AND THIS SLEEP MAKES NO SENSE WHAT THE FUCK

DRUNK SONNET 12

WE ARE A GARBAGE BAG STUFFED WITH BOTTLES AND NO
I CAN PROBABLY JUST HANG THE GARBAGE OUT THE WINDOW
AND LET THE STREET SMELL IT AND WE CAN STILL SMELL IT HERE
I WANT TO GET RID OF EVERYTHING ON THE FLOOR AND IN THE AIR

IN THE BREATH OF THE EVENING I PROBABLY FELT YOU
THAT'S ALL I CAN EVEN SAY TO DESCRIBE IT
I CAN'T—AND SOMEWHERE ELSE I AM SOMEONE ELSE
AND YOU ARE THE SAME WHY CAN'T YOU LEAVE

THAT THERE EXISTS A PLACE FOR YOU AND ME AND ANYONE
DOESN'T MEAN ANYTHING ANYMORE BECAUSE OTHER PLACES YES
I THINK THERE ARE OTHER PLACES TO MOVE ON FROM THIS

I'M JUST AN ASSHOLE WITH FLOWERS HANGING OUT OF IT
BUT EVERYONE STILLS MY FLOWERS AS TURDS
AND WHAT SMELL OF WHAT WAS I SAYING AGAIN, PLEASE?

DRuNK SONNET 13

THE ONLY THING THAT COULD MAYBE SAVE US NOW
IS GETTING OLD TOGETHER AND DYING AND THEN NOTHING
I THINK THAT THIS IS THE TIME FOR US
I HAVE WALKED THROUGH OUR CITY AT NIGHT

IT'S HARD TO IMAGINE CHANGING ANYTHING NOW
BUT WHEN I FALL IN LOVE IN THE FUTURE
WILL I EVEN THINK OF YOU OR WHAT? I DON'T KNOW
WILL YOU EVEN BE A PART OF THAT?

HERE ARE SOME THINGS I'VE SEEN TONIGHT
THAT MAKE ME THINK OF YOU OK:
CAT LITTER, THAT WAS THE FIRST

YOUR PICTURE ON THE INTERNET
WHAT ELSE, I DON'T KNOW, SHOULD I QUIT MYSPACE?
SHOULD CATS EVER PISS AGAIN?

DRUNK SONNET 14

IF ANYONE KNOWS WHAT IS GOING ON EVER THEN HEY
I AM HERE IT WOULD BE NICE TO TALK SOMETIME
INFOMERCIALS HAVE STARTED AND I KIND OF WANT TO DIE
I'M PRETTY SURE THIS ONE IS ACTUALLY FOR A MORGUE

OK SO ACTUALLY IT'S FOR THE BIBLE OR SOMETHING
SO IT'S A COMMERCIAL FOR TRYING TO BE HAPPY OR SOMETHING
BUT I AM NOT HAPPY TONIGHT NO I AM NOT JUST HERE
IF HAPPINESS EVER WORKED THEN HOW—I DON'T KNOW

HAPPINESS IS A LIZARD IN THE SUNLIGHT GETTING WARM
AND THEN IN THE NIGHT BENEATH A ROCK EATING FLIES
AND SWALLOWING THE MEAT OF THE TRASH OF THE DIRT

AH, SO TONIGHT IS A LITTLE DRUNK AND OK OK OK
THAT IS GOOD SO LET ME BE—THERE IS NO LOVE TONIGHT
GOD IS LIKE BONO—SOME DICKWAD NO ONE WILL EVER MEET OR LIKE

DRuNK SONNET 15

NO ONE CAN BE COMPLETE WITHOUT THAT THING
THAT COMPLETES THEM AND MAKES THEM ALIVE
AND IF THAT THING IS NOT LOVE THEY ARE NOT ALIVE
AND I THINK I AM ALIVE BUT THAT LOVE IS ASTRAY

WE STAND PUNCHING WALLS AND THROWING TRASH
ACROSS THE FLOOR LIKE DUST AND IT SOAKS IN
AND WHEN WE CLEAN IT UP WE CAN ONLY THINK
WHERE HAS IT GONE FOR IT TO BE LIKE THIS

AND IF I AM NOT ALIVE LET ME BE FABRIC SOFTENER
OR A LIGHT BULB OR AN OVEN OR SOMETHING OF USE
AND LET ME BE A PART OF SOMEONE'S LIFE

IN A WAY THAT MAKES LIFE EASIER AND BETTER
SOMETHING THAT CAN NEVER BE HARMED OR NOTHING
THAT NO ONE CAN EVER STOP CARING ABOUT OR NEEDING

DRuNK SONNET 16

TOMORROW I COULD BE A PLANT
AND YOU COULD BE A PLANT
AND WE COULD BE NEIGHBORS
IN A FOREST IN SCOTLAND

AND THE SKY COULD RAIN ON US
AND THE WORMS COULD MAKE GOOD DIRT
AND THE DIRT COULD SUSTAIN US
AND OUR LOVE WOULD SMELL LIKE THE EARTH

BUT WE ARE NOT PLANTS
WE ARE NOT WORMS
WE ARE NOT DIRT

WE ARE HUMAN BEINGS
AND WE ARE ARE MISSING THE POINT
AND I'M A LITTLE DRUNK AND YOU'RE A LITTLE DRUNK

DRUNK SONNET 17

I AM NOT STILL THINKING ABOUT YOU, NO
I AM NOT STILL THINKING ABOUT YOU AT ALL
I AM NOT STILL THINKING ABOUT YOU
STILL, I AM NOT AT ALL THINKING ABOUT YOU

NOT THINKING ABOUT YOU, NO I'M NOT
WHAT AM I THINKING ABOUT? NOT YOU
IF I AM THINKING ABOUT ANYTHING, IT'S NOT YOU
YOU ARE NOT A THING I'M THINKING ABOUT

WHAT SHOULD I THINK ABOUT? NOT YOU
WHAT CAN I POSSIBLY THINK ABOUT?
WHAT IS THERE TO THINK ABOUT BUT YOU?

THERE'S PLENTY TO THINK ABOUT IN THIS WORLD
WHAT IN MY LIFE AM I THINKING ABOUT?
I AM NOT THINKING ABOUT YOU, THANK GOD

DRuNK SONNET 18

I'M GOING TO DRINK ALL THE BEER
IN MY APARTMENT TONIGHT
IT'S A LOT AND IT'S GOING TO HURT
AND I ASSURE YOU TOMORROW WILL BE HARD

IF YOU CAN SEE ME RIGHT NOW SAY YES
EVERY DAY WE ARE NICE THINGS
WRAPPED IN A BLANKET ON A COUCH
TRYING TO BE WARM AND EVEN WARMER

THE HEAT IS TURNED UP TO 80
I AM WEARING SWEAT PANTS, A SWEATER
I AM IN A BLANKET, INDOORS

OUTSIDE, BIRDS ARE SWARMING TO THE SOUTH
THEY ARE LEAVING TOGETHER, BEAUTIFULLY
TOMORROW THEY WILL MAYBE BE IN KENTUCKY

DRuNK SONNET 19

I WANT TO BE A DICK TO SOMEONE SOMETIME
I WANT TO KICK SOMEONE'S DICK IN LIKE A DOOR
AND I AM THE SWAT TEAM AND THE DICK HAS A GUN
AND I AM RUSHING IN AND IT WILL PROBABLY HURT

TODAY I ALMOST THREW UP AT WORK
I WAS JUST SITTING THERE AND I HAD TO LEAN FORWARD
AND BREATHE VERY SLOWLY LIKE BIRTHING A GHOST
WE HAVE SO MUCH IN COMMON, I THINK

I HATE BEING ASKED ABOUT JESUS OR GOD
IF I COULD HAVE FAITH IN ANYTHING COULD IT PLEASE BE MYSELF?
INSIDE THERE IS A SMALL CONGREGATION OF LOST MEMORIES

FOR ONCE, I HAVE TREATED MY BODY LIKE A TEMPLE
I HAVE KNELT INSIDE MYSELF AND LOWERED MY HEAD
AND THIS PRAYER ANSWERS ITSELF WITH BLOOD

DRuNK SONNET 20

TONIGHT FEELS EXTREME LIKE HATE CRIMES
I HAVE SET MY COUCH ON FIRE, AND MYSELF
I KNOW IF I STAND UP I WILL JUST SIT AGAIN, EVENTUALLY
AND I WILL BE CLOSER TO THE FLOOR WITH EVERY DRINK

IT'S HARD TO ACCEPT ALL THIS LIFE RUSHING AT ME
I THINK IF I HAD EMPATHIC ABILITIES I WOULD DIE
I WOULD JUST LIE DOWN AND HURT WITH EVERYTHING
I FEEL A LITTLE BIT VULNERABLE RIGHT NOW

I FEEL LIKE HIDING BEHIND THIS LINE
AND THIS LINE ATTEMPTS TO REDIRECT
AND THIS ONE IS A REMINDER OF WHY I AM HIDING

I REGRET HAVING TO TREAT THESE LAST LINES
IN SUCH A HORRIBLE AND LAZY FASHION
BUT I AM DONE WITH THIS POEM

DRuNK SONNET 21

THIS BEER IS GOOD
THIS APARTMENT IS GOOD
NOT HAVING TO GO TO WORK TOMORROW
THAT IS GOOD TOO

WORK IS SOMETIMES GOOD
GOING HOME NEXT MONTH IS GOOD
THE STREET I LIVE ON IS GOOD
THE ROOF ABOVE ME IS GOOD

THE DVD I WAS WATCHING IS GOOD
THE MUSIC I'M LISTENING TO IS GOOD
THIS SWEATER IS GOOD AND KEEPS ME WARM

LIFE CAN BE GOOD IF WE WORK AT IT
WE ARE ALL GOOD IF WE TRY
AND TRYING IS A VERY GOOD THING

DRuNK SONNET 22

I HAVE SO MUCH BEER TO DRINK TONIGHT
MORE BEER THAN I SHOULD PROBABLY DRINK
I AM ALONE AND I WILL DRINK IT ALONE
THIS IS MY COMMUNION

DRINKING BEER MAKES ME FEEL LIKE THAT HYMN
ABOUT LOVE POURING DOWN ON MY FACE
AND LEAVING ME A VERY GRATEFUL PUDDLE
OF LIFE IN SEARCH OF MEANING LIKE THERE IS MEANING

GOING TO PARTIES CAN BE A LOT LIKE SLAVERY
YOU HAVE TO TALK TO PEOPLE YOU CAN'T STAND
AND MAKE THEM THINK YOU LIKE THEM

YOU HAVE TO DANCE AND PRETEND TO LIKE IT
AND IF YOU DON'T DO THESE THINGS
YOU WILL GET PUNCHED IN THE FACE

DRuNK SONNET 23

I AM PROBABLY GOING TO MASTURBATE TONIGHT
IT'S JUST GOING TO HAPPEN, I THINK
UNLESS I GET TOO DRUNK BEFORE IT HAPPENS
THAT'S HAPPENED TO ME BEFORE TOO

I'VE MADE PLANS TO MASTURBATE
AND THEN I'VE BROKEN THOSE PLANS
BECAUSE I'M TOO DRUNK AND TIRED
AND MY DICK WANTS SOME SLEEP

I HAD A DREAM ABOUT DESTINY'S CHILD LAST NIGHT
THEY WERE NAKED AND UNDERWATER
AND IT WAS LIKE IT WAS ON TV OR SOMETHING

WATER WAS PUSHING THEIR BODIES BACK AND FORTH
THE WORD "GOS" KEPT APPEARING IN FRONT OF ME
IT WAS A STRANGE DREAM, BUT NICE

DRUNK SONNET 24

IF I AM NOT A HEART ATTACK
THEN I AM A SHARK ATTACK
I JUST BIT SOME LEG OFF
OF I DON'T KNOW WHAT

I LIVE MY LIFE LIKE I EAT MY BURRITOS
WITHOUT REMORSE, WITH HEART, LIKE A SHARK
ATTACKING A BUILDING IN THE SKY OF THE OCEAN
THE ONE THAT EXISTS FOR MOMENTS LIKE THESE

WHERE THE SPINNING IS NOT DISEASE
WHERE THE CHAMBERS OF THE HEART
ARE ALL FILLED WITH N64 CONSOLES

AND MY VEINS ARE THE N64 GAMING SYSTEM
I CANNOT BE CONSOLED RIGHT NOW
I AM IN GOLDENEYE. I CARRY THE GOLDEN GUN

DRUNK SONNET 25

I WANT TO BE POOR FOREVER
IF I COULD KEEP MYSELF ALIVE AND CONTENT
THEN THAT'S ALL I NEED
EXCESS MONEY WOULD BE SPENT UNWISELY

I WOULD BUY A SATELLITE AND BROADCAST DISEASE
I WOULD BUY A SHADOW AND STITCH IT TO THE SUN
I WOULD BURY MONEY AND TRY TO GROW A MONEY TREE
FUCK ALL Y'ALL I CAN PRETTY MUCH DO ANYTHING

I WOULD BUY A THIRD WORLD COUNTRY AND ENSLAVE IT
I WOULD SOAK UP THE OCEAN WITH CASH
I WOULD SHADOWBOX A HORSE AND THEN EAT COINS

EVERYTHING IS BETTER AS A POSSIBILITY
ACTUALLY, MOST OF THOSE THINGS WOULD SUCK
$$

DRuNK SONNET 26

I HAVE NOTHING REALLY INSIDE ME TO GIVE
IT'S ALL AN EMPTY ROOM WITH GREY CARPET
I REMEMBER DONATING TOYS AT THE FIRE DEPT.
WHEN I WAS A KID AND I WANTED THOSE TOYS

BEING A KID WAS THE MOST RETARDED SHIT EVER
BECAUSE KIDS TURN INTO ADULTS AND THAT SHIT'S WHACK
I FALL OVER DRUNK MORE THAN EVER NOW THAT I'M AN ADULT
I WANT MY FACE KICKED IN MORE THAN EVER NOW

MOST EVERYTHING STOPS WORKING EVENTUALLY
EVEN THE SUN WILL STOP WORKING, AND MY BODY
I CAN'T THINK OF ANYTHING THAT WON'T BREAK SOME DAY

I COULD RIDE A DONKEY UP A MOUNTAIN UNTIL THE DONKEY DIES
OR THE MOUNTAIN ERODES AND SLAPS FACES WITH DIRT
AND BABIES START SNORTING COCAINE HELL YES

DRUNK SONNET 27

IN THE FUTURE I DIED AND IT WAS FUN
IT WAS LIKE A ROCKING CHAIR WITH AN OLD LADY
GETTING ANGRY AT MIDNIGHT TRAINS IN JULY
IT WAS AWESOME AND IT REALLY SUCKED

WHEN YOU SEE YOUR BODY QUIT ITSELF
IT'S LIKE WATCHING A CAR WRECK IN THE RURAL SOUTH
FROM AN EXTREME DISTANCE IN 1923
AND ALL THE WORLD'S TOMMY GUNS ARE IN MOURNING

I COULD LOVE YOU MORE THAN EVER RIGHT NOW
THAT'S THE WAY IT IS WHEN YOU DIE, I THINK
I COULD LOVE YOU MORE THAN EVER

IT JUST ALL COMES OUT AND IT'S THERE
MY BELIEF IN YOU OR DISBELIEF IN YOU
IT DOESN'T MATTER EITHER WAY

DRuNK SONNET 28

LET'S HAVE A BABY PLEASE
LET'S HAVE A BABY AND WATCH IT GROW
LET'S VIDEOTAPE THE BABY GROWING
LET'S TIMEWARP THE VIDEO

LET'S WATCH THE BABY GROW AT INTENSE SPEEDS
LET'S WATCH IT GO FROM ZERO TO THREE YEARS IN 30 SECONDS
LET'S TOUCH OUR FACES TOGETHER AND KISS
LET'S UNDERSTAND THE WATER THAT KEEPS US ALIVE

LET'S TELL OURSELVES THAT WE ARE NO MISTAKE
LET'S FALL DOWN INTO A PILE OF DUCK BLANKETS
LET'S HAVE SOME FUN FINALLY AND LOVE SOMETHING

LET'S GET AWESOME TOGETHER AND MAKE LIFE GOOD
LET'S HAVE THIS, ALL OF THIS
LET'S NOT BE SAD OR ALONE ANYMORE PLEASE

DRuNK SONNET 29

ONE WAY TO THINK ABOUT DYING IS LIKE A HUG
I THINK THAT DEATH, THAT DUDE IN BLACK ROBES
COULD POSSIBLY UNDERSTAND THAT LIFE IS HARD
OTHERWISE, HE PROBABLY WOULD'VE QUIT BY NOW

NO ONE COULD TAKE LIFE AWAY DAILY
WITHOUT THINKING IT WAS A GOOD OR MERCIFUL THING
I ACTUALLY BELIEVE THAT HE FEELS FOR US
WHEN WE DIE, DEATH WILL COMFORT US FOR A BIT

AND THEN THAT'S IT—GOOD NIGHT EVERYONE
HIS ARMS WILL WRAP US LIKE PET SNAKES WITH ALZHEIMERS
HIS ARMS ARE ARMS THAT TRULY CARE

OR ARMS THAT GIVE THE ILLUSION OF CARING
BUT IT WILL BE ENOUGH FOR US
HE WILL DROP HIS SCYTHE AT OUR FEET

DRUNK SONNET 30

I WISH I HAD A LOVE POEM TO WRITE
BUT IT'S NOT THERE RIGHT NOW
LISTENING TO LOVE SONGS AT NIGHT
IS A TERRIBLE HABIT TO BREAK

THE WORST THING ABOUT LOVE SONGS
IS PROBABLY THE WAY THAT THEY MAKE LOVE EASY
EASY OR EVEN SENSIBLE
LOVE IS HARDER THAN NOISE MUSIC

4/4 TIME OR 3/4 TIME OR WHATEVER IT TAKES
I COULD USE A LITTLE OF THAT STRUCTURE
SO I COULD TEAR IT APART OR SOMETHING

I LIKE SONGS THAT SORT OF FALL APART A LITTLE
SONGS THAT MAKE ME FALL APART A LITTLE
SONGS THAT MAKE THE CEILING FALL APART A LITTLE

DRuNK SONNET 31

LISTENING TO LUKE HENLEY
IS POSSIBLY THE MOST BEAUTIFUL THING EVER
LUKE'S SONGS ARE HONEST IN THE WAY
THAT A BULLET IS HONEST WHEN IT GRAZES YOUR TEMPLE

AND YOU ARE OK BUT BLEEDING A LITTLE
YOUR TEMPLE WILL SCAB AND BLOOD WILL STAY IN YOU
BUT YOU HAVE NO IDEA WHO SHOT YOU
BUT YOU HAVE A GOOD IDEA

AND YOU JUST WANT SOMEONE THERE
AND NO ONE IS THERE
AND LUKE'S GUITAR IS YOUR FAVORITE DRUNK SCAR

I LIKE LOOKING AT MY SCARS AND FEELING THEM
I CAN NEVER FEEL SCARS BUT I FEEL THEM ANYWAY
I WANT AN EARTHQUAKE TO DAMAGE THIS PLANET TONIGHT

DRuNK SONNET 32

I HATE THAT I NEED DEPRESSION TO FEEL LIKE MYSELF
I DON'T KNOW LIFE WITHOUT IT
COME ON, WHAT AM I EVEN DOING?
IS HAPPINESS A GOOD THING?

DEPRESSION FEELS LIKE A BEARHUG FROM A BEAR
AND THE BEAR CAN'T SPEAK BUT ITS WARM, WET FUR SPEAKS
AND IT SAYS, I LOVE YOU, I AM GOING TO MAUL YOU TONIGHT
AND GOD IS JUST THE DREAM OF SOME OLD TOOTHLESS MAN

IT'S LIKE FALLING OUT OF YOUR OWN ASSHOLE
AND YOU ARE A PREMATURE BIRTH, SMALL AND GREY
HARDLY WORTH KEEPING

I THINK LOVING SOMEONE IS A GOOD CURE
BEER IS A GOOD DISTRACTION
I DON'T KNOW ANYTHING ELSE

DRuNK SONNET 33

I DON'T KNOW MANY PEOPLE WHO HAVE DIED
BUT I KNOW PEOPLE WHO WILL DIE SOON
WHAT I MEAN, IS I AM GOING
TO SOME FUNERALS SOON

TODAY I WATCHED A KID PUNCH SPIDERS
INTO A WALL AND SMASH THEM TO DEATH
HE WAS LAUGHING. I LISTENED TO HIS FISTS
SMASH AGAINST THE WALL—I JUST WATCHED

HIS STEP-DAD ONCE THREW A JAR OF SPIDERS
INTO HIS BED—HE WAS FIVE
SPIDERS TERRIFY HIM

ANOTHER OF HIS STEP-DADS PUT TURDS
IN HIS BED—HE WAS A LITTLE OLDER
I DON'T KNOW IF HE'S AFRAID OF TURDS

DRuNK SONNET 34

MY FAVORITE BIBLE VERSE GOES LIKE THIS:
THE UNIVERSE SAT ALL AROUND US AND WEPT
IT JUST HAPPENED AND NOW WE ARE HERE

LIFE IS NOT A MISTAKE, MORE LIKE A MILLION CAR PILE-UP
LIKE AN INSIDE JOKE OR SOMETHING
BETWEEN YOU AND THAT PLACE IN THE TREES
BEHIND THE STOPLIGHT THAT YOU LOOK AT EVERY NIGHT
ON YOUR WAY HOME FROM WORK WHEN THE CITY IS ASLEEP

THE TREES ARE ALL LIKE, THE AIR FEELS NICE
AND YOU ARE ALL LIKE, YOU WILL BE FELLED ONE DAY
BY WEATHER OR BY CHAINSAW, JUST WAIT, YOU'LL SEE

AND THE TREE IS ALL, BITCH PLEASE, SHUT UP
AND THE SKY IS ALL, I HAVE NOTHING TO SAY
AND THE UNIVERSE IS ALL, ...

DRUNK SONNET 35

IF WE WERE BOTH LITTLE PIECES OF SHIT
SWIMMING IN THE SEWER WITH ALL THE OTHER SHIT
THEN I HAVE NO REASON TO BELIEVE I WOULD KNOW YOU
ALL US SHIT IS REALLY THE SAME—GONE FOREVER

THE BODIES WE CAME FROM, OUR HOMES
GODDAMMIT, WHAT AM I EVEN DOING HERE
WE ARE DISSOLVING BELOW THE CITY
THE MANHOLES ARE OUR CHIMNEYS

IF SOME RIVER TAKES US AWAY FROM HERE
THEN THAT WILL BE A MERCIFUL RIVER
AND I WILL LOVE IT, COLD AND ALL

IF SOME OCEAN SWALLOWS US
THEN THAT WOULD BE PERFECT
US SO SMALL AND ALL

DRuNK SONNET 36

TRYING TO HELP ANYONE WITH ANYTHING IS TIRING
I HAVE NEVER MET ANYONE WHO DOESN'T NEED HELP
AND I NEED HELP AND YOU NEED HELP AND THEY NEED IT TOO
SO WHY CAN'T WE ALL HELP OURSELVES

WHY CAN'T WE ALL DRINK FROM THE SAME WATERS
WHY ARE THERE ALWAYS CROCODILES BENEATH THE SURFACE
IF THERE COULD BE A RAIN THAT JUST SOAKED US
AND IT BEAT US DOWN WE COULD MAYBE MOVE ON

IF THE RAIN COULD MAKE THE DIRT INTO MUD
AND THE WEEDS INTO VEGETABLES
OR EVEN JUST MORE WEEDS TO COVER THE EARTH

IT'S MORE THAN WE HAD BEFORE
IT'S POSSIBLE THAT OUR LIVES WILL NEVER TOUCH
IF THIS IS IT, LET THIS BE IT

DRUNK SONNET 37

IF I THINK, OH! GOOD IDEA!
I WALK AWAY AND IDEA JUST DIES
IF LOVE, LOVE JUST GETS PUSHED AWAY

ALL EARTH GETS PUMMELED BY EARTH
AND THAT MAKES EARTH BEAUTIFUL
IF ALL THE WHEAT SUDDENLY CAUGHT ON FIRE
ALL THAT CRACKLING WOULD SET US MARCHING

ALL THE BEAUTY THAT CAN POSSIBLY EXIST!
PLEASE LET THIS BE MY LAST POEM EVER!
BUT IT WILL NEVER BE, I KNOW

THIS ALL KEEPS ON AND KEEPS ON
I WILL STILL KEEP TRYING AND MOVING
WILL YOU STILL KEEP TRYING AND MOVING?

DRUNK SONNET 38

I'M SURE ALL THE HOSPITALS HAVE OPEN BEDS TONIGHT
I'M SURE YOUR BED IS OPEN TONIGHT
LIKE MY BED IS OPEN TONIGHT
I MEAN, EVEN IF I'M SLEEPING ON MY COUCH

WITH MY SHEETS ALL DIRTY, I DON'T KNOW
IS THIS BED EVEN MINE NOW?
THIS FLOOR IS MINE NOW
THIS PLACE IS MINE NOW

I WANT TO WATCH A DVD THAT MAKES ME LAUGH
I WANT TO FORGET ALL THAT HAPPENS
I WANT THE A-HA! MOMENT OF MY LIFE TO COME

IT HASN'T COME YET BUT HEY WHATEVER
IF YOU'RE THERE OR NOT THEN WHATEVER
IT WAS GOOD BUT NOW LIFE IS ALL, WHAT IS THIS

DRUNK SONNET 39

I HAVE FOUR CLOSETS NOW
WHAT THE FUCK AM I GOING TO DO
WITH FOUR CLOSETS
MY LIFE IS TOO SMALL FOR THIS PLACE

I NEED MORE SHIT TO MAKE IT SEEM A GOOD SIZE
I WANT TO DRAW ON THE WALLS
I WANT THE TREES ON THE STREET
TO PUSH THROUGH THE WINDOWS

I WANT THE TREES TO DROP LEAVES ON MY CARPET
I NEED SOMEONE WITH VERY FEW POSSESSIONS TO MOVE IN
AND TO STAY AWAY FROM ME AND BE QUIET

ACTUALLY, THERE IS AN AVAILABLE APT. ABOVE ME
MOVE INTO THAT PLACE AND LIFE WILL BE GREAT
FOR BOTH OF US, IT WILL BE PARTY AND HELL YES CONSTANTLY

DRUNK SONNET 40

I JUST FARTED AND IT SMELLED LIKE DUST
I THINK THAT MEANS I'M GETTING OLD
FUCK, I'M ONLY 23 YEARS OLD
24 IN A MONTH, YESTERDAY

WHAT HAPPENS NOW IS I SHOULD GET A TATTOO
NOT REALLY, BUT I SHOULD TATTOO A CATERPILLAR
I SHOULD TATTOO MYSELF PRISON STYLE
I SHOULD MY DEATH SENTENCE BROCCOLI

I LOVE LIFE A LOT MOST OF THE TIME
I LOVE THE PEOPLE I KNOW
I LOVE WATCHING THE WORLD GET OLDER BY DAY

I CAN'T BELIEVE THAT CERTAIN PEOPLE ARE DEAD THOUGH
CHRIS FARLEY, FRANK O'HARA, GOD, WILLIE MAYS
HOW DOES DEATH EVEN HAPPEN?

DRuNK SONNET 41

THIS IS MY LAST BEER OF THE NIGHT
MY MISSION IS ALMOST COMPLETE
THAT SHIT IS ALMOST ALL DRANK UP
I CUT MY FINGER UP TRYING TO OPEN IT

I DON'T HAVE A BOTTLE OPENER YET, JUST A COUNTER
I'VE ALWAYS FELT THAT BLEEDING
WAS A BEAUTIFUL FEELING AND I LOVE IT
REALIZING THAT THE BODY IS MORE THAN SKIN AND FUR

GODDAMMIT, THERE IS SO MUCH INSIDE ME
THE BLOOD, THE BONES, THE MUSCLE
THE VEINS, THE FAT, THE ORGANS

I CAN'T BELIEVE MY SKIN CAN CONTAIN IT ALL
IT CAN BE OPENED SO EASILY
AND IT CAN LET OUT SO MUCH

DRuNK SONNET 42

HEY! TOMORROW WILL BE BEAUTIFUL I THINK!
WHY NOT! I WILL GET MY LIFE UNDER CONTROL!
I WILL LOVE MYSELF AGAIN!
I WILL BE BRUTAL TOWARD ALL THAT OPPOSE ME!

MY HEART WILL BE A BEATING THING AND I WILL LET IT!
MY LUNGS WILL PUSH AIR THROUGH ME! HOLY SHIT!
I DON'T EVEN FUCKING KNOW WHAT I'M DOING NOW!
I'M JUST HERE AND THAT'S ENOUGH FOR ME OK!

THE WALLS ARE MINE! AND THE FLOOR IS MINE!
THIS BLACK AS SHIT SKY IS MINE! AND IT IS FOREVER!
THIS WALL IS MINE! THIS CEILING IS MINE!

THIS HALLWAY IS MINE AND I CAN WALK IT ALL NIGHT!
THIS SINK IS MINE AND IT IS MINE TO FILL WITH SORROW!
I HAVE MY OWN LIFE TO PUSH TOWARD ANY END OR ANY BEGINNING!

DRUNK SONNET 43

IF I LOVE ANYONE NOW IT'S—I DON'T KNOW
LOVE ALWAYS ENDS IN TERRIBLE WAYS
THEY SAY IT HAS TO GET WORSE BEFORE IT GETS BETTER
BUT IT ALSO GETS GOOD BEFORE IT GETS WORSE

AND NOW I'M FINDING MY WAY BACK
BUT I DON'T BELIEVE IN "GOOD" ANYMORE
I ONLY BELIEVE IN LIVING AND CONTINUING
AND THAT'S GOOD ENOUGH FOR NOW

THERE'S A BIKE TRAIL NEAR HERE
AND I'M GOING TO RIDE IT SOON
I MIGHT RIDE ACROSS THE TRACKS

ABOVE THE RIVER AND LOOK DOWN AT THE WATER
OR WALK ACROSS THE TRACKS AND STARE AT THE ROCKS
AND SAY HELL YES TO ALL THIS, NO MATTER WHAT

DRuNK SONNET 44

IN SOME WAYS I KNOW
THAT EVERYTHING IS ALREADY DONE
AND THAT'S WHY ALL MY LIGHTS ARE ON

I'M AFRAID OF NOT SEEING AGAIN
IN THAT WAY THAT I SAW YOU THAT NIGHT
DRUNK, AND UNBELIEVABLE

AND I LOVED YOU
AND I KNEW IT
THAT WAS IT

NOW MY HEART IS AN UPRISING
AND YOU ARE NOT A PART OF IT

I DON'T KNOW WHAT I STAND FOR, AND YOU

WHAT DO YOU EVEN STAND FOR NOW
I COULDN'T STAND IF I TRIED

DRUNK SONNET 45

THE MOON IS LIKE A BAYONET IN THE CHEST SOMETIMES
I SAY THAT BECAUSE TONIGHT IS BLOOD

I JUST WANT TO FALL IN LOVE AGAIN
THE CARPET LOOKS LIKE GRAVEL
I NEED TO KEEP MY HEAD UP TONIGHT

YOUR WONDERFUL LIGHT ABOVE
THE STREET IS HARD AND COLD AND ALL
IT HAS EVERYTHING FOR MY CAR

THE SIDEWALK HAS ENOUGH FOR MY SHOES
THE MOON ENOUGH FOR THE LEAVES OUTSIDE
TO BE NOTICED AND TO SHINE LIKE THEY DO

I COULD PRACTICALLY RIP MYSELF APART
AND WHAT WOULD I EVEN FIND BUT YOUR LOVE
THAT I'VE SAVED UP LIKE CRUMBS

DRUNK SONNET 46

I'D LOVE TO PUNCH THROUGH YOUR HEART LIKE DRYWALL
AND YOU WOULD CHARGE ME A DAMAGE DEPOSIT
AND I WOULD GLADLY PAY IT

I THINK THE DUST WOULD SCATTER MY FACE APART
LIKE I WAS LEAVING BUT YOU HAVE LEFT ALREADY
I AM WATCHING MY FEELINGS GROW SMALLER AND SMALLER

OF ALL I'VE GIVEN I DON'T THINK I'VE RECEIVED EVEN HALF
WE ARE ALL CHEATED
I AM POCKETS OUT AT THE TOLLBOOTH OF THE HEART

MMMMMM … THIS IS THAT SOUND OSUDFA
I KNOW THAT WE BOTH CARED AND EVEN LOVED
WE ARE TWO DIFFERENT THINGS YOU KNOW

I LICKED THE SPOONS THAT WE HAD SCOOPED INTO OUR HEARTS
AND I GAVE YOU TWO SCOOPS EVERY TIME—I WASN'T CHEAP

DRUNK SONNET 47

GOD WHAT IS IT THAT DRAWS ME
EVERYTHING IS BASICALLY OVER
IT HAS BEEN OVER SINCE EVER AT THIS POINT

I DON'T BELIEVE THAT LIFE IS MEANT TO BE CRUEL
IT'S JUST THAT FLOOD LEVELS RISE QUICKLY
AND USUALLY IT'S THE POOR THAT GET LEVELED ANYWAY

OH, THE THINGS I COULD SAY TO YOU
THIS HEART GETS LEVELED FAST

IT'S JUST ANOTHER DISASTER THAT I'M TRYING TO ESCAPE
THESE LIGHTS ARE TOO BRIGHT AND I AM WEARING OUT

BASICALLY, I AM DONE
AND YOU ARE ALSO POSSIBLY DONE

AND I HAVE A BURRITO IN THE MICROWAVE
THAT IS ALSO POSSIBLY DONE

DRuNK SONNET 48

I AM NOT HOPEFUL OF ANYTHING ANYMORE
THE BLANKETS THAT HOLD ME COULD BE EMPTY, WHATEVER
AND I AM HOPEFUL INSIDE LIKE A SICK CHILD

WHEN I LOOKED INTO THE SUN TODAY I WAS BLINDED
AND MY EYES SCALED UP LIKE TWIN LIZARD FETUSES
TELL ME YOU HAVE NOT HYPNOTIZED ME OR SOMETHING

TELL ME THE SUN WILL STILL BE THERE TOMORROW

I WANT THE HOPE INSIDE ME TO DECIDE SOMETHING
JUST TAKE ME SOMEWHERE WITHOUT MY CONSENT
I AM NOTHING; I AM A WEAK CHILD TRIPPING DOWN THE STAIRS

I WILL EAT THE FUTURE AND THE PAST
MY STOMACH TURNS, BUT IT IS NOTHING
AND WHAT ABOUT YOU?
I WANT TO EAT YOUR HEART

DRUNK SONNET 49

YOU ALWAYS ASKED IF MY POEMS WERE ABOUT YOU
I ALWAYS SAID NO OR MADE UP AN EXCUSE

ALRIGHT
THIS IS #49
POEM-WISE YOU ARE ALMOST OVER THE HILL
SOON YOU WILL BE DEAD

I CAN'T TELL YOU HOW MUCH IT HURTS ME
TO THINK OF YOU THAT WAY
BUT I NEED YOU GONE

THESE ARE MY POEMS AND I NEED THEM

WHY ARE YOU EVEN IN THEM?

IT'S LIKE THOSE CAVE PAINTERS COULD ONLY THINK OF THE HERDS
AND COULD ONLY THINK OF THE HUNT AND THE LIFE GAINED
AND I CAN ONLY THINK OF YOU

DRuNK SONNET 50

I WANT TO PUT MY FIST INSIDE YOUR CHEST
AND LET IT SETTLE LIKE A HEART
AND I WILL CLENCH MY FINGERS TO PUMP YOUR BLOOD

AND I WILL OPEN MY FINGERS AND LIFT MY HAND
INTO YOUR SKULL AND I WILL CARRY YOUR BRAIN
INTO YOUR STOMACH AND LET YOUR ACIDS DIGEST YOUR BRAIN

YOUR HEART, BRAIN, MY HAND, EVERYTHING

I DON'T KNOW IF IT MATTERS TO YOU, BUT I TRIED

I WOULD'VE LET MY FACE BURN UP, MY THROAT, STOMACH, SOUL

WHAT DO YOU EVEN FEEL WHEN YOU THINK OF ME?

A VACANT SPACE IN THE BED
A PASSING SATELLITE DISAPPEARING IN THE NIGHT

NOW IT IS CONSTANT
I WILL HOVER ABOVE YOU, SO PLEASE STAND STILL

DRUNK SONNET 51

THIS ONE IS NOT ABOUT YOU
PLEASE STOP READING
THIS IS FOR THE GIRL AT THE LAUNDROMAT TONIGHT

I WANTED YOU TO WALK OVER TO ME
AND SAY HELLO LIKE YOU WERE OPEN TO ANYTHING
LIKE YOU WOULD'VE STAYED IN WITH ME AND HOPED

LIKE WE COULD'VE LISTENED TO THE WEAKERTHANS
THAT'S REALLY ALL I WANTED TO DO, AND DRINK
TO HEAR WORDS LIKE, "YOU SAID TRUE MEANING
WOULD BE DYING WITH YOU AND THOUGH I WANTED TO

I DID NOT SMILE."
WE COULD'VE LOOKED AT EACH OTHER, EXPRESSIONLESS
LIKE EXPRESSIONS COULD EVER DO JUSTICE
TO WHAT THIS MOMENT TRULY REQUIRES

DRUNK SONNET 52

LET'S PLANT BUSHES IN OUR CHESTS
AND LET THEM EXPAND SOME UNTIL WE ARE HAPPY AGAIN
I THINK THE ONLY THING TO MAKE US HAPPY
WOULD BE SENDING OUR EMOTIONS VIA SATELLITE
TO SOME SMALL PLANET WITH ONLY MOLD FOR LIFE

CURRENTLY, I AM IN A PERIOD OF STASIS
EVERYTHING AROUND ME IS GOING ONE WAY OR ANOTHER
AND QUITE BEAUTIFUL REALLY
IT REMINDS ME OF A KESTREL SWOOPING LOW TO THE GROUND

AND RISING LIKE A BLANK PROMISE I KNOW
WILL BE FULFILLED, NO MATTER HOW TRIVIAL

BUT AS FOR ME, I AM A ROCK AMONGST A BED OF PINES
AND MY ONLY LOVE IS THE RAIN AND THE WIND

DRuNK SONNET 53

I HOPE ALL THE LOVE I'VE EVER FELT GETS RUPTURED
LIKE A COMET BREAKING THE ATMOSPHERE TONIGHT
I HOPE A LITTLE BOY IN RUSSIA IS AFRAID OF WHAT IS HAPPENING
I HOPE WE CAN LEARN TO CARE AGAIN, THAT IS ALL

I THINK ABOUT IT NOW AND HOW IT NEVER MADE SENSE
HOW WE ARE TINY BANQUETS FOR A RETIRED JANITOR
ATTENDED ONLY BY THE RATS AND THE MOPS
THAT HE ATTENDED TO IN HIS AMAZING CAREER

HE KEPT THREE STORIES CLEANER THAN I CAN KEEP MY OWN HEART
GODDAMMIT, HOW DOES THIS EVEN WORK

AND THE LITTLE BOY IN RUSSIA IS JUST CRYING IN BED
LIKE A LITTLE GIRL IN IOWA, THE NIGHT AFTER HER BIRTHDAY

I FEEL LIKE A SMALL TRIBE OF HALLELUJAHS
GETTING SENT UP TONIGHT, STUCK IN THE RAFTERS, ECHOING

DRUNK ESSAY TO SAY HEY
DANIEL BAILEY

FOR KENDRA, MIKE, AND ELIZABETH SIMULTANEOUSLY

I DO NOT FEEL AS LOUD IN THESE CAPS AS I FELT FOUR YEARS AGO WRITING THIS SHIT THAT YOU READ RIGHT HERE IN THIS BOOK. THAT IS NOT TO SAY THAT I DON'T FEEL LOUD BUT I FEEL MUTED LIKE THE UNIVERSE PUT ME IN ITS ARMS FOR A MOMENT AND SCREAMED QUIETLY, "DAN IT IS ALL OK IT IS OK YOU ARE HERE AND YOUR BODY WILL REMAIN HERE WHEN YOU ARE GONE WHAT YOU NEED TO WORK ON IS INSIDE YOU JUST PLEASE MAKE THAT AS BEAUTIFUL AS YOU CAN MAKE IT" AND THAT'S WHAT I HOPE I HAVE BEEN WORKING ON SINCE I WROTE THE DRUNK SONNETS IN THE LATE MONTHS OF 2008. I STILL FEEL ANGRY AND I STILL FEEL SAD AT TIMES BUT I ALSO FEEL LIKE I AM LUCKY TO BE WHERE I AM, TO HAVE MET THE PEOPLE I HAVE MET, AND DONE WHATEVER WITH WHATEVER I HAVE HAD NEAR ME JOGGING INTO MY LIFE OR BRAIN OR WHAT.

I LIKE IT.

THIS BOOK THAT YOU ARE READING CAME AFTER A

SHITTY BREAK UP WHERE I ENDED UP WITHOUT A PLACE TO STAY. THAT'S NOT TRUE. BUT YES IT IS. MY BROTHER JOHN WELCOMED ME BECAUSE I AM HIS BROTHER AND BECAUSE I LOVE HIM LIKE A MILLION UNBROKEN LIGHT BULBS AND I HOPE HE FEELS THAT WAY TOO. I WROTE THE FIRST HALF THERE. THEN I WROTE THE SECOND HALF WHEN I MOVED TO DOWNTOWN MUNCIE, INDIANA, INTO A CHEAPASS TWO BEDROOM APARTMENT AND WROTE THE SECOND HALF OF THE DRUNK SONNETS INTO A WORD DOC AND FELT LIKE I HAD COMPLETED MY SORROW. IT IS BEAUTIFUL TO COMPLETE SORROW EVEN IF COMPLETING SORROW DOES NOT COMPLETE SADNESS. AT LEAST THE SORROW WAS GONE.

I WAS THEN RESCUED BY MY FRIEND AND COWORKER ADAM BRIDGES WHO I CONSIDER TO THIS DAY TO BE ONE OF THE MOST COMPLETE AND BEAUTIFUL FRIENDS THAT I HAVE EVER HAD THE BLESSING TO KNOW. ALL HE DID WAS CONVINCE ME TO FINALLY START GOING OUT AGAIN. AND SO I EVENTUALLY DID AND HAD THE BEST SPRING AND SUMMER OF MY LIFE JUST GETTING DRUNK ALMOST EVERY NIGHT AND LEARNING TO ENJOY PEOPLE AS PEOPLE.

I WENT ON TO GET MY MFA. WHICH I PROBABLY SHOULDN'T HAVE DONE. I DON'T KNOW OR CARE ABOUT ALL OF THAT. I WILL SKIP THAT FOREVER. IT IS NOT EVEN WORTH A MONTAGE IN THE FILM OF MY LIFE. THE CRITICS

WILL SHIT INTO THE HELL OF THIS MOVIE SCREAMING "MORE EDUCATION. MORE EDUCATION. UNDO THE MOMENT OF BLISS. WE WANT MORE FORMAL EDUCATION. WHERE IS THE ROBIN WILLIAMS TO DANIEL BAILEY'S [SOME KID IN THAT MOVIE. I HAVE NEVER ACTUALLY WATCHED DEAD POETS SOCIETY. I DON'T CARE.]."

I AM HAPPY NOW IN THAT I HAVE A BEAUTIFUL RELATIONSHIP GOING ON TWO AND A HALF YEARS AND WE BIRTHED AN AMAZING DOG NAMED ELAINE OUT OF THESE HERE DENVER MOUNTAINS UNDERNEATH THIS HEARTLESS SKY WITH NO WEATHER.

FUGGIT MY FRIENDS.

I WANT TO SAY THAT I HAVE FOUND IT. BUT I HAVE FOUND NOTHING. I WORK AT A MENTAL HOSPITAL ON THE ADOLESCENT UNIT. MY JOB IS TO KEEP PATIENTS SAFE. I MAKE LESS THAN SOME ADOLESCENT PATIENTS HAVE CLAIMED TO EARN AT GARDENING JOBS AND THAT IS OK.

IT WOULD BE COOL TO LOOK INSIDE MY BODY AND SEE HOW

EVERYTHING WORKS

TO FILL IT ALL WITH FOOD DYE AND WATCH THE BLOOD CIRCULATE LIKE WEATHER.

NOW THAT I AM HAPPY I CAN SEND A BALLOON INTO THE SKY AND LET IT

GREET THE LORD

I AM HUNGRY

I KNEW I SHOULD'VE LET DAVE BERRY WRITE THIS ESSAY

I AM A FOREGONE CONCLUSION

WHEN MY HEART IS IN MY HANDS IT TOO BECOMES A WITNESS

TO THE BEAUTY OF THIS ALL OF THIS

I WOULD LIKE TO THANK EVERYONE ON THIS EARLY PAGE OF THIS ESSAY (I CAN FEEL IT LASTING FOR MANY MORE PAGES).

I WOULD LIKE TO THANK MY PARENTS FOR BEING THE MOST KIND AND LOVING PARENTS POSSIBLE AND FOR LETTING ME EXIST IN THIS WORLD THAT IS MOSTLY AMAZING. I WOULD LIKE TO THANK MY BROTHERS [ESPECIALLY JOHN FOR COUCHING ME AND DEALING WITH ME IN MY SHIT] FOR GROWING WITH ME AND FOR SO MANY THINGS THAT ARE ONLY TRUE IN OUR HEARTS. I WOULD LIKE TO THANK MEGAN FOR BREAKING UP WITH ME, IT WAS THE RIGHT THING TO DO, YOU ARE AN AMAZING PERSON, AND LOOK WHAT GOOD IT DID FOR ME, I HOPE YOU ARE DOING WELL TOO. I WOULD LIKE TO THANK ADAM BRIDGES FOR PICKING ME UP OFF THE FLOOR AND BEING THE BEST PERSON YOU CAN BE (I DON'T THINK YOU COULD EVER BE LESS) AND FOR

INTRODUCING ME TO B-MAN. I WOULD LIKE TO THANK SHAUN GANNON FOR BEING AND FOR ANCHORING ME AMONGST THIS WORLD OF LIT PEOPLE. I WOULD LIKE TO THANK MIKE YOUNG FOR SO MANY THINGS BUT MOSTLY FOR SAYING THAT THIS SHIT DOESN'T SUCK AND SENDING IT OUT. DUDE YOU MAKE ME FEEL LIKE I AM A TINY STONE AND YOU ARE DAVID AND YOU SHOT ME RIGHT THROUGH GOLIATH'S HEAD. I WOULD ALSO LIKE TO THANK LESLIE NANCE BECAUSE I ONLY REMEMBER YOU BEING POSITIVE AND SUPPORTIVE THROUGH MY SHIT DAYS AND YOU ARE FAMILY.

I WOULD ESPECIALLY LIKE TO THANK KENDRA GRANT MALONE. WE STARTED THIS SHIT WHEN IT WAS A NEW THING TO BE TRUE. WE EMAILED POEMS TO EACH OTHER. I REMEMBER WRITING MANY OF THOSE FIRST DRUNK POEMS WHILE AT MY PARENTS' HOUSE ON CHRISTMAS BREAK AND READING YOUR RESPONSES AND WORD DOC-ING MY OWN POEMS BACK TO YOU. AND I REMEMBER FEELING THAT YOUR POEMS WERE ALWAYS BETTER THAN MINE. AND I STILL FEEL LIKE I AM BEING SHOWN A NEW PART OF THE WORLD EVERY TIME I READ A NEW POEM OF YOURS. BUT STILL WE STARTED THIS SHIT. YOU ARE THE BEST. ORVILLE AND WILBUR DAWG. THE REDENBACHERS OF POETRY. COOKIES FOR THE LITERATE WORLD. COOKIES OVER KITTY HAWK.

I WOULD ALSO LIKE TO SMACK MANY PEOPLE BUT

THIS IS NOT THE PLACE.

I ONLY FEEL LIKE I CAN SPEAK ABOUT WHAT IT IS.
HOW DO I YELL LOUDER THAN CAPS THAT "IT IS GOOD."
BECAUSE IT IS.

I CAN ONLY THINK OF RACEHORSES RIGHT NOW.

RACEHORSE SONNET

I CAN ONLY THINK OF RACEHORSES RIGHT NOW
GALLOPING THROUGH THE GODDAMN CURVE OF THE FENCE
CRUSHING THE MECHANICAL RABBIT AND KNOCKING OVER
A LANTERN INTO THE HAY OF THE BARN

IT IS SO COOL TO LOOK UP AND SEE A CHANDELIER
TO SEE SIX LIGHT BULBS UNLIT
TO LOOK OVER AT THE LIGHTSWITCH AND KNOW
THAT I AM THOSE BULBS COMPLETELY

LIGHTSWITCHES INSIDE OF ME
I AM THE SMALLNESS OF THE NIGHT
TRYING TO BE BIG IN THE MOMENT OF ITS ARRIVAL
BUT HAVING NO JUDGE OR HAVING NO SPEECH

I GIVE THIS MOMENT ITS BREATH
HEAR THE CHURN OF THE FAN

WHAT GLADNESS I GIVE THE WORLD IS NOT ENOUGH.
I WANT TO GIVE THE WORLD ALL MY GLADNESS. I WANT
TO GLADLOCK THE WORLD AWAY INSIDE ME. BOOM.
BUT REALLY I LOVE THAT, GROWING UP, AND BECAUSE
MY DAD WORKED (AND STILL WORKS) FOR DOW, WE HAD

AN ENTIRE CLOSET FILLED WITH ZIPLOC BAGS (DOW ONCE OWNED ZIPLOC I THINK). I STILL HAVE SOME ZIPLOC BAGS OR RECENTLY HAD FROM THE LATE 80S. I WOULD LIKE TO REVISIT THAT CLOSET AND THE DARTBOARD NEXT TO IT AND REMOVE DARTS AND SEND THEM AND THEIR BROKEN FEATHERS INTO THE ALUMINUM PIPES OF THE CEILING NOW THAT SOME RANDOM PERSON WHO RUINED MY MOM'S AMAZING LANDSCAPING LIVES THERE.

BUT SERIOUSLY MY MOM MADE THAT YARD BEAUTIFUL. STONES AND GIANT ROCKS, DUSTY MILLERS AND JAPANESE MAPLES, SNAPDRAGONS AND ROWS OF PINES THAT LED UP TO THE ALREADY EXISTING CHERRY TREE. THE HOUSE WAS SOLD TO SOME FUCKERS WHO REPLACED ALL THAT WITH SMALL SHRUBS LINING THE EDGE OF THE CONCRETE PORCH LIKE CEMETERIES LINING THE EDGE OF A BATTLEFIELD.

BWAH.

I JUST SWITCHED FROM WHISKEY NEAT TO BEER. I WROTE THE CRUNK SONNETS ON BEER. WHATEVER. FUCK THAT SHIT. I MOSTLY DRANK BASS. A LOT OF BASS. MY DAD LOVES BASS AND SO DO I. IT'S A GREAT BEER. I DRANK IT BECAUSE IT WAS CHEAP AND EASY TO DRINK AND DRINKING IN MASS IT WAS GOOD AND TASTED GOOD. I REMEMBER DRINKING BASS AND USING THE ENCYCLOPEDIA PROGRAM BUILT IN TO MY COMPUTER TO SEARCH FOR SONNETS AND FINDING A SONNET BY

ELIZABETH BARRETT BROWNING I THINK, AND I TRIED
TO TRANSLATE ONE OF HER POEMS INTO MY OWN VOICE
AND I COULDN'T AND THAT POEM DOESN'T EXIST. BUT
I WILL TRY TO TRANSLATE ONE OF HER SONNETS NOW,
WHICHEVER COMES UP FIRST ON GOOGLE.

SONNET 43 BY ELIZABETH BARRETT BROWNING

IF I HAD TO PUT MY LOVE INTO NUMBERS IT WOULD BE 1,000,000
I LOVE YOU LIKE A REALLY TALL DEEP PIECE OF BREAD
MY SOUL HAS HANDS IT CAN FEEL EVERYTHING IF BLIND
ALSO FUCK POLITICS AND BEING

I WANT MY EVERY DAY TO BE LIKE MY LOVE
I WANT IT TO BE QUIET AND TO LIGHT A CANDLE WITH MY SUN
MY LOVE IS REAL THOUGH IT IS THE REAL THING
IT IS SO REAL

I WISH I WAS A HAMMER OR A DOOR JAMB OR SOMETHING
AND I WISH I WAS LIKE A BABY MADE NEW TO YOU AND ME
IF I EVER GET LOST KILL ME FOR REAL THOUGH KILL ME
MY HEART IS ONE MILLION BREATHS UPON A DEAD DEAD FIRE

AND OF ALL THE BREATH THE BREATHING OF YOU
LET'S WASTE US NOW LET'S PIKACHU

OK SO THAT WAS A POEM THAT ENDED STUPIDLY IN ITS
LAST WORD WHICH IS HOW A POEM SHOULD MAYBE END.
MAYBE THAT'S WHY THE RED WHEELBARROW ENDED ON
CHICKENS. I THINK I AM PARAPHRASING PETER DAVIS ON
THAT, WHO I WOULD ALSO LIKE TO THANK FOR SHOWING

THE BEAUTY OF POETRY, HOW IT CAN SAVE LIVES AND CREATE WORLDS SIMULTANEOUSLY. IT IS STUPID HOW MUCH I AM.

TODAY I WALKED MY DOG AROUND THE BLOCK. TODAY AN INSANE WOMAN CONTINUED TO LIVE IN HER BED WHICH SHE HAS SET UP BEHIND THE DUMPSTER ACROSS THE ALLEY. TODAY ELIZABETH AND I SPENT APPROXIMATELY $75 ON WEDDING GIFTS TO REMIND SOME PEOPLE THEY ARE IN LOVE OR SOMETHING LIKE THAT. TOMORROW I WILL GO TO WORK AND ATTEMPT TO KEEP SOME MENTALLY ILL PEOPLE SAFE FOR ONE MORE DAY. THAT IS MY JOB. I WORK AT A MENTAL HOSPITAL. I KEEP MENTALLY ILL PEOPLE SAFE AND LEAD GROUPS THAT I AM NOT TRAINED TO LEAD. I GET PAID APPROXIMATELY $11.50 AN HOUR TO DO THIS BUT WITH AN ADDITIONAL $2 ON THE WEEKENDS. I GET HEALTH INSURANCE THOUGH. DESPITE MY SHITTY PAY I FEEL LUCKY.

WHO THE FUCK AM I TO COMPLAIN?

I WISH I COULD JUST EAT MYSELF INTO THE NEXT LIFE. INSTEAD I HAVE TO LIVE MYSELF THERE. THAT IS OK THOUGH. THAT IS HOW IT SHOULD BE.

I WISH I COULD SHIT MY SHADOW BACK INTO MY OWN BODY.

I ALWAYS HEAR THE EARTH SAYING THAT IT CANNOT TAKE THIS DEATH AND THEN IN MY OWN HOPEFUL I HEAR IT SAY SOME SHIT ABOUT HOW THAT DEATH BIRTHS LIFE

OR SOME SHIT. AND THEN EARTH IS ALL "I DON'T CARE."

NUB WAGON BY BOOM BABIEZ.

"DIDDA LING DING DING DING DING DING DING" COULD BE AN ALTERNATE TITLE OF THE MOVIE (OR BOOK [FOR SEAN LOVELACE]) DELIVERANCE.

ALSO I MISS MARK CLEMENTS'S LAUGH.

SHAKE YOUR FISTS AT A STATUE OF MONTEL.

I WANT TO BE THE WHOLE WORLD BUT I THINK THAT IS ALSO EVERYONE ELSE'S PROBLEM TOO

WE ALL NEED TO JUST CHILL THE SHIT OUT AND HAVE A DREAM ABOUT GETTING SHOT OFF A BRIDGE THAT GOES OVER A RAVINE IN THE CENTRAL AMERICAN JUNGLE AND THEN YOU WAKE UP AND YOUR NECK HURTS BECAUSE THAT'S WHERE YOU WERE SHOT.

I HAD THAT DREAM WHEN I WAS LIKE 10 BUT APPARENTLY IT DIDN'T TAKE BECAUSE I STILL SUCK AS A HUMAN BEING.

DEAR LORD, PLEASE SHOOT ME THE FUCK OFF A SUPER HIGH CENTRAL AMERICAN JUNGLE BRIDGE AND PLEASE SHOOT ME IN THE NECK WHILE I AM TIED TO A CHAIR AND PLEASE MAKE SURE TO KICK ME REAL HARD TOWARD THE BOTTOM OF THE RAVINE TO MAKE SURE THAT I DIE BUT PLEASE LET ME LIVE THE REST OF MY LIFE FROM THIS MOMENT ONWARD. PLEASE LET ME FINISH THIS ESSAY AND THEN PLEASE LET ME GO TO BED TO ELIZABETH AND WAKE UP TOMORROW SO SHE CAN KISS

ME BEFORE SHE GOES TO WORK AND THEN SHE CAN COME HOME EARLY BECAUSE THE AIR CONDITIONING AT HER WORK IS BROKEN AND THEN WE CAN HAVE PART OF A DAY TOGETHER BEFORE I GO TO WORK.

I WOULD LIKE TO THANK EVERYONE WHO KNOWS ME. BECAUSE.

WHO THINKS THEY KNOW ME?

MY FAVORITE POEM EVER IS BY FRANK O'HARA. IT BEGINS, "I AM STUCK IN TRAFFIC IN A TAXI CAB / WHICH IS TYPICAL" AND THAT LINE "WHICH IS TYPICAL" IS SOMETHING LIKE WHAT ELIZABETH ALWAYS SAYS. EXCEPT SHE ALWAYS SAYS "TYPICAL" AFTER ANYTHING SHE DEEMS TYPICAL, AND I ALWAYS I FINISH IT IN MY HEAD "AND NOT JUST OF MODERN LIFE" BECAUSE THAT'S HOW THIS BEAUTIFUL POEM CONTINUES.

SONNET PLUS 4

I WANT MADLY TO WRITE SOMETHING AS BEAUTIFUL AS A POEM
BUT I AM ALWAYS IN BETWEEN NOW AND MY MOMENT
AND IF GOD DEEMS ME SO THEN CONSIDER ME DEEMED
WHAT AM I BUT A MOLLUSK UNDER PRESSURE OF WAVES

OH MY FRIENDS HOW STUPID IT IS TO BE
IF NOT LACKING THEN IT IS LIKE SUDSING THE SUN
IT IS TOTALLY LIKE THAT I SAY TO YOU
I SAY THAT AS I SUDS THE WORLD UNTIL BLING

I CANNOT SHALLOW THE SMALL OF ME
I CANNOT CONTINUE TO RUN
IF HEAVEN IS A PLACE IT IS A PLACE WITH MORE
THAN IS PROMISED BY WHAT I UNDERSTAND

I THINK THAT MIGHT BE A REASON TO KEEP
I WOULD LIKE TO CRUSH MY EMOTIONAL PAST
I WOULD LIKE TO CRUSH MY EMOTIONAL FUTURE
I WANT TO BE THE SONG I SING AS GOD FEEDS ME TO SATAN

WHAT IS HELL IS LIKE A BABY WITH A HEART
BABIES HAVE NO HEART, JUST MORE BABY HEARTS

I ALWAYS WANT TO SAY "GOLF INTO A HORSE'S BUTT" LIKE THE HORSE'S BUTT IS A RUNWAY AND THAT ALWAYS SEEMS LIKE THE MOST RELIGIOUS THING I COULD EVER POSSIBLY DO.

NOTHING MATTERS.

NOTHING MATTERS UNLESS IT DOES MATTER, WHICH NOT MUCH ACTUALLY DOES.

I GUESS LOVING MATTERS. AND SO DOES GIVING A FUCK.

WHEN I STOP GIVING A FUCK IS WHEN I THROW MYSELF INTO THE RAVINE. I AM NOT THERE AND I AM A LONG WAY OFF.

I WOULD STILL LIKE TO EAT THE HAM OF MY OWN BODY.

PLEASE DON'T JUDGE ME FOR THAT. I WOULD FOR REAL LIKE TO KNOW WHAT I WOULD TASTE LIKE ALL

COOKED UP FOR CHRISTMAS.

HORSES ARE FUCKING STUPID THOUGH. ANGELS
SEEMS LIKE THE HIGHLIGHTS OF GOD'S HAIR.

LET ME FINISH THIS BEER REAL QUICK QUICK. AND
THEN PEE. AND THEN GET A NEW BEER. THEN I WILL
WRITE YOU A POEM ABOUT ANGELS.

ALSO I JUST HEARD MY DOG SIGH FROM HER CRATE.
IT WAS A REALLY BEAUTIFUL SIGH. PLEASE REMEMBER
HOW BEAUTIFUL SIGHS CAN BE.

HERE IS A POEM (SONNET) ABOUT ANGELS:

I GIVE SO MANY SHITS O HOLY ANUS O BLACK SKY
PLEASE IF I DROWN LET ME DROWN IN BEAUTY
WELL AFTER THAT LINE I LOOK UPON EVERYTHING
I GAVE LIFE A REAL THINK AND AS ALWAYS I AM

WHAT FUCK FUCK FUCK FUCK FUCK FUCKING FUCK
IT IS SO AWFUL TO THINK I CANNOT ACHIEVE ULTIMATE
    PROFANITY
TO OFFEND THE MOST GODAWFUL PART OF ME
TO RAPE MY HEART WHOLE AND LET ITS JIZZ DROWN MY LOVE

OH MY GOD LIKE A BIRTHDAY CAKE EAT ME
OH MY GOD LIKE A ROAD FLARE LOSE ME
OH MY GOD LIKE A DIVING RING LET ME DROWN
OH TELL ME AT THE BOTTOM OF THE POOL

HOW NOTHING IS GOODNESS. HOW LOVE IS HURT
BUT HOW MUCH OF HURT OH HOW MUCH YES

I AM DRUNK AND GETTING DRUNKER. WHAT I WANT TO DO IS KEEP SITTING IN THIS FEELING FOREVER. MAYBE NOT FOREVER. AT LEAST UNTIL SOMETHING VALIDATES, WHICH I GUESS COULD BE THIS SENTENCE. THAT SENTENCE SAYS, "HEY YOU WERE VALIDATED IN THAT YOU FELT GOOD IN WRITING THAT." BUT IT'S NOT ALL ABOUT THAT. IT'S ABOUT THE LOVING AND WHO YOU LOVE. IT'S ABOUT WHO YOU YOURSELF ARE WITHIN THAT LOVE.

I WANT TO END THIS ESSAY THERE. BECAUSE IT FEELS RIGHT, BUT I HAVE TO FINISH THIS BEER, OTHERWISE THIS ESSAY WOULD GO AGAINST THE DRUNKNESS, WHICH IS "FINISH THAT BEER," AT LEAST IN MY HEAD IT WAS.

I'M GLAD THAT'S NOT ME NOW. I LIKE TO HAVE A GLASS OR TWO OF WHISKEY. I LIKE TO DRINK THAT AND HAVE MY LIFE. THIS IS TOO MUCH. THREE GLASSES OF WHISKEY AND THREE BEERS. I LIKE TO HAVE MY LIFE. I WOULD LIKE TO SIT WITH MY LIFE FOR A FEW AND SEE WHAT IS GOING ON. I WOULD LIKE TO SEE IF IT SEES WHAT I SEE, WHICH I DON'T KNOW THAT IS.

AHEM.

AHEM. AHEM.

SAYING "AHEM" SEEMS LIKE A REALLY BEAUTIFUL PERSON INSIDE A COMMUNITY OF IDIOTS WISHING HE OR SHE COULD JUST SAY "AMEN" TO A BUNCH OF BEAUTIFUL SAYINGS.

I SAY AHEM INSIDE MY OWN MIND CONSTANTLY.

GODDAMN BUT HELLO. GODDAMN IS A HELLO.

I WANT TO SWING MY CHARIOT SO LOW THAT THE AXLE DRAGS ON THE GROUND AND THE HOT HOT SAND THAT IT LIGHTS ALL OF ROME ON FIRE.

I WANT TO SMOKE THE CRACK OF MY OWN AFTERBIRTH.

AND I DON'T WANT TO BE BEAUTIFUL.

I WANT TO BE LIKE THE SMOKE THAT LETS PEOPLE KNOW THAT THERE IS TOO MUCH FIRE.

AFTERBIRTH SONNET (FINAL SONNET)

I HOPE TO DILDO GOD THAT THIS IS THE LAST SONNET EVER
IF THIS IS NOT THE LAST SONNET EVER
THEN LET ALL POETS BE DILDOED TO DEATH FOREVER
IF NOT THEN JUST STRAIGHT UP FUCK THOSE ANUSES

MEOW MEOW MEOW IT WOULD BE COOL TO BE TRIPPING RIGHT
    NOW
IT WOULD BE COOL TO FEEL REAL POSITIVE AND WHATNOT
AND TO SEE THE LIGHT SLOWLY BEND ON YOUR FACE
OH TO LISTEN TO BOZ SCAGGS RIGHT NOW

LORD LET MY TEAM BE A CHAMPIONSHIP TEAM FOR ONCE
VIKINGS OR PACERS OR NUGGETS OR US
RED WINGS HAVE WON MANY BUT LET THEM WIN ANEW
OH MY GOD I'M SORRY I'M SORRY I'M SORRY FOR THIS

I WANT TO BE SMOKE IF THERE IS ENOUGH FIRE
IF NOT THE AFTERBIRTH OF FIRE O SMILE

SONNETS ARE DONE I WILL NEVER WRITE ANOTHER. I LOVE THEM AND WILL ALSO NEVER WRITE ANOTHER DRUNK POEM I HOPE. THIS IS ALL DONE. THANK YOU ALL I LOVE YOU. I LOVE YOU ALL THE BEST. AND IN MY LOVE OF YOU I EXTINGUISH WHATEVER IT IS I FEEL OF MYSELF. THAT IS WHAT IT IS TO LOVE. THAT IS WHAT IT IS TO BE A FIRE. A FIRE IS A FORCE THAT EXTINGUISHES ALL THAT IT CONSUMES AND IT CONSUMES ONLY ITS OWN SELF.

OMG WHAT ALTJLEKWJADFS.VM,X

CAN PLEASE BE YOU IF YOU BE ME?

I WOULD LIKE TO SAY GOD BLESS ALL OF YOU IF YOU ARE ALIVE STILL AND READING THIS. I WOULD LIKE TO SAY THAT IF YOU ARE CREATING SOMETHING, IMAGES OR WORDS, THAT YOU ARE CREATING SOMETHING AND THAT IS SOMETHING WORTHWHILE. PLEASE KEEP CREATING UNTIL YOU FEEL YOU HAVE CREATED THE MOST BEAUTIFUL THING IN THE UNIVERSE THAT NO ONE ELSE CAN POSSIBLY RECREATE. I HAVE NOT CREATED THAT THING YET. THOUGH I OFTEN FEEL PREGNANT IN A WAY THAT SUGGESTS BEAUTY BUT IT OFTEN SAYS "HELLO I AM JUST A GIANT FART" AND IN THAT WAY I CONTINUE WITH THIS. I CONTINUE SAYING "I LOVE YOU" TO NOTHING, HOPING THAT NOTHING GIVES ME ITS WORLD, HOPING THAT NOTHING WELCOMES ME THROUGH ITS DOORS AND INTO ITS STUPID FAMILY, BUT THEN I REMEMBER MY OWN FAMILY AND THEN I WISH

NOTHING BUT TO STAY. I REMEMBER GETTING HIT IN THE FACE WITH A GHOSTBUSTERS FILMSTRIP. I REMEMBER THE EVERYTHING OF OUR RIDES TO GEORGIA AND BACK AND THE NOTHING OF MY NIGHTS ALONE WATCHING COMEDY CENTRAL. I WANT TO EAT THE HORSE OUT OF ME, PUT IT ON A GODDAMN GOLF TEE AND SMACK THAT SHIT INTO A NEW SPACE WHERE BAPTISM IS NOT EVEN A POSSIBILITY. I FEEL A NEWNESS RIGHT NOW AS I HAVE FELT A NEWNESS BEFORE, BUT THIS TIME I CHOOSE TO KEEP IT REAL.

FUCK THE NEW. FUCK THE OLD.

I FEEL KIND OF BAD THAT IT IS 3:18 AM AND I NOW HAVE TO TRY TO SNEAK INTO BED AND NOT WAKE ELIZABETH. THOUGH I SHOULD DEFINITELY DRINK SOME WATER AND TAKE A COUPLE IBUPROFEN BEFORE I DO THAT.

GODDAMN YOU, MIKE YOUNG, FOR ASKING ME TO COME UP WITH CONTENT FOR THIS EDITION.

JK.

REALLY, I LOVE YOU SO MUCH FOR THIS. AND RYAN CALL, WHO USED TO BE THE ASSOCIATE EDITOR OF MAGIC HELICOPTER. IT'S NOW TYLER GOBBLE. YOU ARE BOTH GREAT.

BUT MIKE YOUNG, THIS IS ALL BECAUSE OF YOUR BELIEF IN ME, WHICH IS AS MUCH AS I'VE EVER NEEDED.

DANIEL BAILEY is the author of *Hallelujah, Giant Space Wolf* (Mammoth Editions, 2012), *Gather Me* (Scrambler Books, 2013), and numerous e-books. He lives in Denver, CO, where he edits *New World Poetry* and works on Champion of the Couch Press with Elizabeth Taddonio.

Made in the USA
Monee, IL
07 July 2026

56549086R00056